Hardanger Embroidery

Translated from the Italian by Natalia Tizón
Photographs by Alberto Bertoldi, Giuseppe Pisacane

Library of Congress Cataloging-in-Publication Data

Ciotti, Donatella.
  [Sfilature. English]
  Hardanger embroidery / Donatella Ciotti.
    p. cm.
  Includes index.
  ISBN-13: 978-1-4027-3227-0
  ISBN-10: 1-4027-3227-9
  1. Hardanger needlework. I. Title.

TT787.C56 2006
746.44—dc22

                          2006005456

Published in 2006 by Sterling Publishing Co., Inc.
387 Park Avenue South, New York, NY 10016
© 2003 by RCS Libri S.p.A., Milano
First published in Italian: *Sfilature*
English translation copyright © 2006 by Sterling Publishing Co., Inc.

Distributed in Canada by Sterling Publishing
c/o Canadian Manda Group, 165 Dufferin Street,
Toronto, Ontario, Canada M6K 3H6
Distributed in the United Kingdom by GMC Distribution Services,
Castle Place, 166 High Street, Lewes, East Sussex, England BN7 1XU
Distributed in Australia by Capricorn Link (Australia) Pty. Ltd.
P.O. Box 704, Windsor, NSW 2756, Australia

Printed in China

Sterling ISBN-13: 978-1-4027-3227-0
        ISBN-10: 1-4027-3227-9

For information about custom editions, special sales, premium
and corporate purchases, please contact Sterling Special Sales
Department at 800-805-5489 or specialsales@sterlingpub.com.

Donatella Ciotti

Hardanger

Embroidery

Sterling Publishing Co., Inc.

New York

Table of Contents

Introduction

Hardanger embroidery is usually done on even-weave fabrics (fabrics with even warp and weft). The edges of the bare spaces left after pulling the threads are embroidered to maintain their shape.

The hemstitch used in Hardanger embroidery is similar to other types of withdrawn-thread embroidery stitches and openwork. Both are done by counting threads and then pulling threads from the fabrics used.

The number of threads to pull out or to group in a stitch varies, depending on the type of fabric used. The lighter the fabric, the more threads are grouped.

Typically, the hemstitch is done on the wrong side of the work.

Threads can be pulled out in a horizontal or a vertical direction. It is important to secure the

ends of the pulled section with festoon or cording stitching. To work all around a piece, you can also pull threads both horizontally and vertically. In this case, you would need to fill in the now bare intersection of the threads at the corners. These empty corners can be worked using block, wheel or spider stitches.

There are a few things you should consider before starting your project. The fabric selected must be evenly woven and the threads should be easy to count. A very compact fabric will make it difficult to count the threads. (Every project in this book indicates the number of threads to pull out.)

The threads used in Hardanger embroidery are typically #25 and pearl cotton #80 (heavier and shinier) for most of the work, and #8 for the finishing borders.

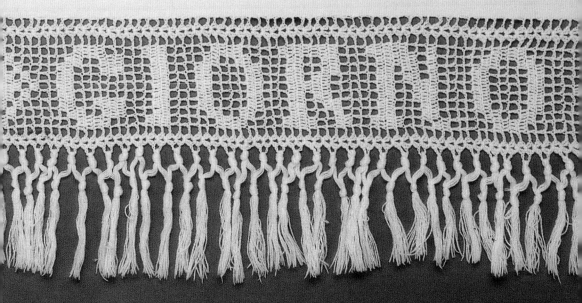

Crochet border on a hand towel embroidered with a hemstitch point.

Tools and Threads

Thimble

Small sharp scissors

Bent tip or stork scissors

Pearl cotton
embroidery thread
#8 and 5

Embroidery thread
#20, 25, 30, and 35

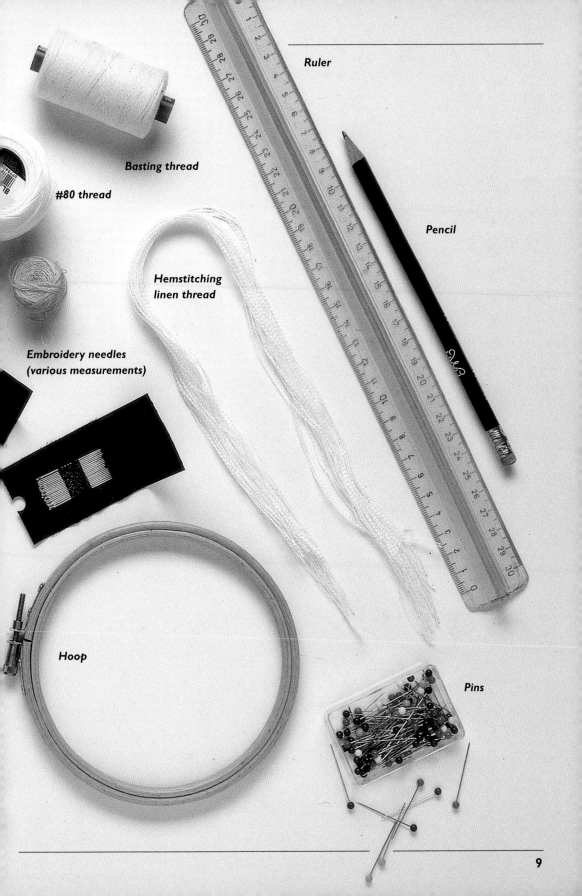

Basting thread

#80 thread

Ruler

Pencil

Hemstitching
linen thread

Embroidery needles
(various measurements)

Hoop

Pins

Fabrics

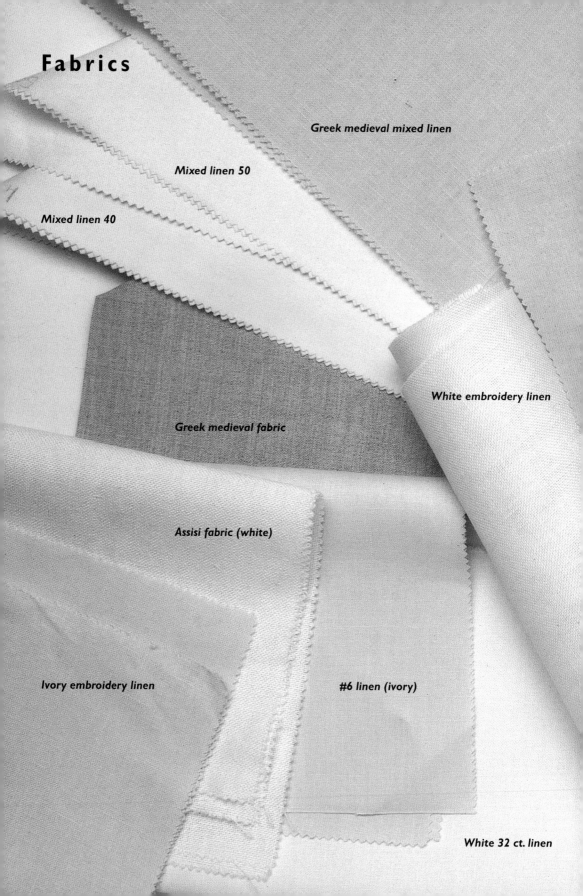

Greek medieval mixed linen

Mixed linen 50

Mixed linen 40

Greek medieval fabric

White embroidery linen

Assisi fabric (white)

Ivory embroidery linen

#6 linen (ivory)

White 32 ct. linen

Country

#6 linen

Double tenax (white and color)

#4 linen (white and color)

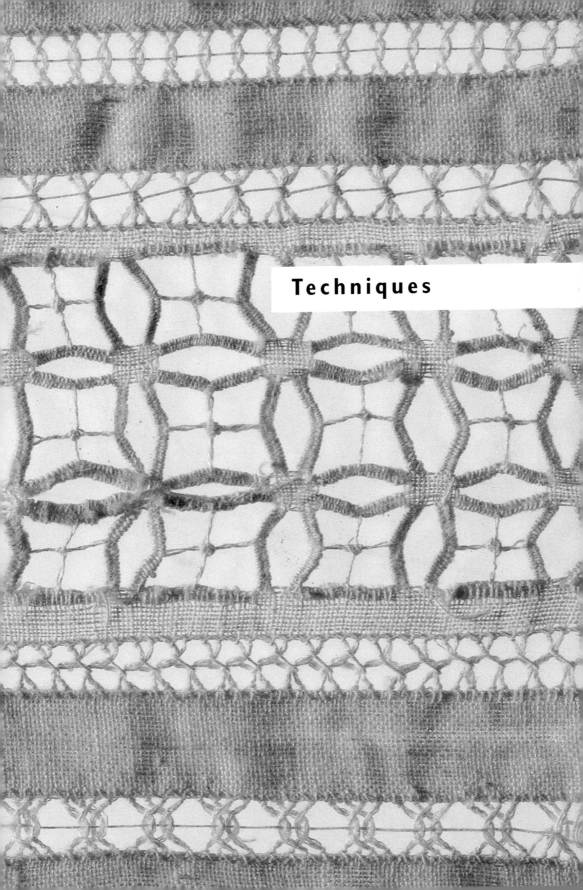

Techniques

Making the Corners

When working with towels, handkerchiefs or similar projects, it is important to create borders with mitered corners and to follow the border properly in order to finish the embroidery correctly. The first step is to determine the desired measurement, double it, and add 1 cm to that number. For example, if you intend to create a 2-cm border, you will need to count 5 cm of fabric.

Straighten the fabric in order to even out the threads. Remove 1 thread at approximately 1 cm from each edge. This will be the first fold of the fabric.

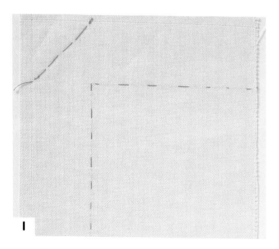

1 With contrasting thread, mark a border line 4 cm from the first pulled thread. If you decide to do a hemstitch, pull 3 or 4 threads. It is important always to pull the threads within the basted line, away from the border area, until the pulled threads form a frame for your work. With contrasting thread, stitch a 45° diagonal line across the corner, always beginning at the first pulled thread. You can use a ruler to help trace the diagonal line.

2 Fold the top half of hemmed corner over, right sides together and with fold passing through the basted corner and matching side edges, making a triangle. Backstitch both layers together along diagonal basting line from fold to the first pulled thread. Trim off corner 5 mm beyond the backstitches.

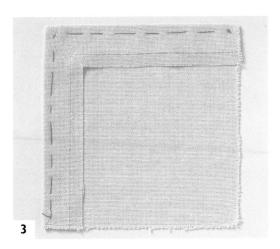

3 Fold inner border to the wrong side. The mitered corner you just sewed should lie flat and the corner should make a sharp angle. You may use scissors to help turn the fabric in the corner. With the fabric folded on the wrong side, baste along the outer folded edge.

4 Fold under the centimeter of fabric marked by the first pulled thread and hem it. This will be the interior fold of the border.

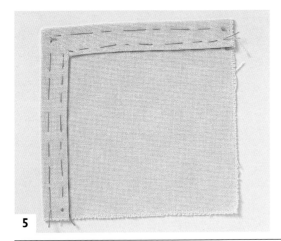

5–6 After you finish the hem, continue pulling the thread. If you would like to pull threads that are very close to the border, you must calculate the height of the pattern, including the pulled threads, to ensure you do not go into the border area. Pull the necessary

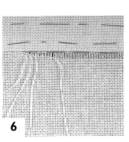

threads. At a corner, draw the thread you are pulling back on itself and secure it. You are ready to start the hemstitching.

Pulling Threads

The purpose of this technique is to achieve transparency. The fabric becomes lighter and, at the same time, the pulled threads will form beautiful patterns. Some of the motifs typically done in this type of embroidery actually reinforce the fabric. Before you start sewing, you will need to become familiar with the technique to pull threads.

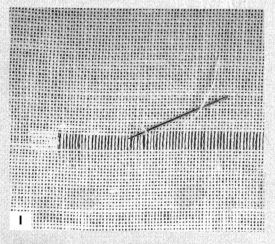

1 Before you pull threads, it is important to ensure that the fabric you are using has weft and warp, with an even weave pattern. You must also verify that the number of weft and warp threads is the same. Cut 1 thread in the center of the area you would like to pull, and use a needle to pull the thread carefully.

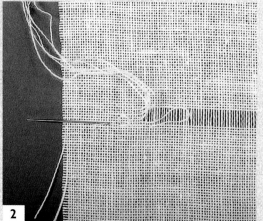

1

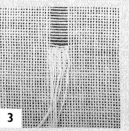

2–3 When you get to the edge of the border you would like to pull, thread the needle with the pulled thread and weave it into the fabric to secure it. Leave the rest of the thread loose on the opposite side of the work for now. At the end of your project, you will cut all the leftover threads.

2

3

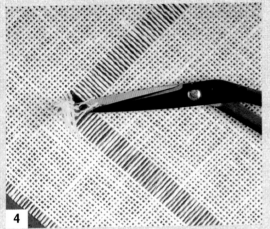

4 When working with corners, you may find it helpful to use bent tip or stork scissors to cut the thread without cutting the fabric. If you cut the fabric, it will be difficult to mend it. You can secure the cut threads either by folding them onto themselves or by doing a small hem.

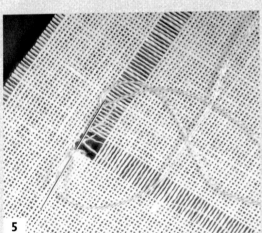

5 On the opposite side of the fabric, make a buttonhole stitch, always sewing from top to bottom and without stretching the fabric. Pass the thread through the fabric, and at every stitch, pull the thread to make the stitch. Repeat this procedure until you complete the desired area.

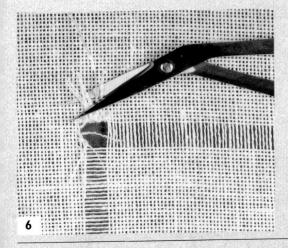

6 Once you have completed the border, cut the leftover thread.

SIMPLE HEMSTITCH

To avoid errors, before beginning to cut threads, you must mark the beginning and the end of the project using a contrasting thread. Begin to cut the threads at the center of the work area. Pull the threads up to within a few centimeters from the beginning and end marks of the area, so that you have enough space to secure them with a cording or festoon border.

Do not wash the fabric before cutting the threads. Otherwise, it could become too thick, and it will be difficult to cut the threads. Once you have finished the project, you may wash the fabric and bleach it so that the fabric and the thread achieve the same shade of white.

I   Cut 3 or 4 threads (depending on the type of fabric) and, working on the wrong side of the fabric, start by doing a border stitch. You should only be able to see the loop around the bar and a perpendicular thread to that loop on the right side of the fabric. Work from left to right. Take a group of threads (in this example, we have pulled out 4 threads and we are taking 3 vertical threads for each group) and make a bar by sewing a stitch horizontally from right to left. On the right of that stitch, do a vertical stitch, passing the needle from top to bottom and taking 2 threads of the fabric. Repeat this procedure. When you reach the end of the work area, you may take 2 threads of the fabric and border and secure the cut threads. To do this, make sure you prepare and hem the border before beginning the work.

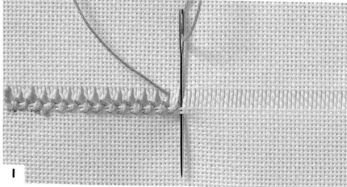

I

ZIGZAG HEMSTITCH

1 Pull the threads horizontally and work from left to right on the wrong side of the fabric. It is very important to work on an even number of threads for each column or bar, so that you can easily divide this number.

2 Once you have finished the hemstitch on one edge of the cut area, turn the fabric and proceed to complete the hemstitch on the opposite edge. Take half of the existing bar and half of the next bar and group them together, creating a "zigzag" effect.

If you prefer, you can also work on the right side of the fabric. Using a contrasting thread will highlight this pattern.

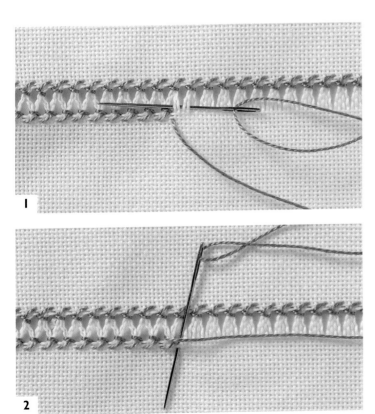

BARS WITH KNOT STITCHING

This pattern is a variation of openwork stitching. The knot stitches can be created in one or more passes to create different motifs.

We recommend working on the wrong side of the fabric so you can move from one bar onto the next without showing the knot from the knot stitch.

1 Pull the threads (in this case, 6 threads) and work the hemstitch at the top and at the bottom of the work area.

2 Working from right to left, connect two bars at a time with a knot stitch at the center, wrapping the thread over, then under the bars as shown.

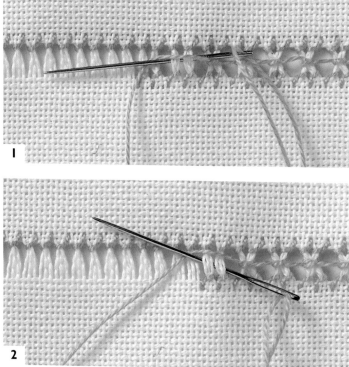

HEMSTITCH WITH LINKED BARS

1–2 Pull 10 threads (or a larger number of threads if you are working with a thin weave fabric). Working on the wrong side of the fabric, create bars by openwork stitching the top and the bottom of the work area. Each bar should have three threads. Work from right to left. Position the thread at the center of the bars to link the bars as follows: Working across the rows of bars, starting at the right end, skip the first bar, slide the needle from left to right under the second bar, then right to left under the first (skipped) bar and the second bar, pull yarn tightly so the second bar twists over the first to link them and so the center thread is taut. Continue across, skipping the next bar, working to the right under the following bar, then to the left under the skipped bar, and so on across each pair of bars.

If you prefer, work left to right across row, as in photograph 2.

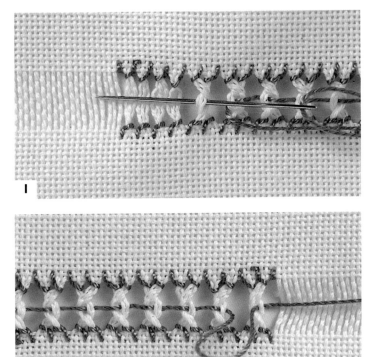

1

2

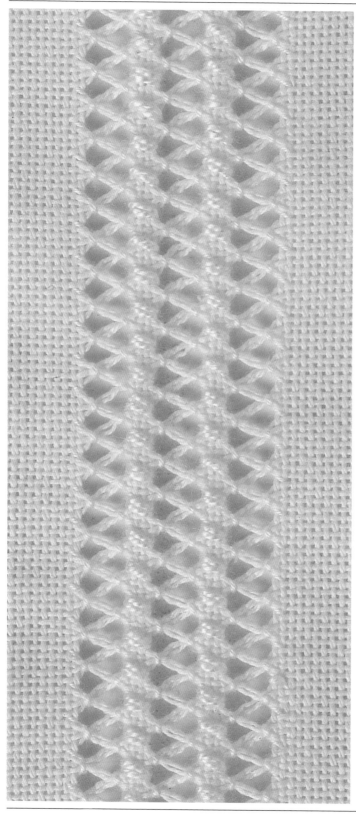

HEMSTITCH WITH ALTERNATING COLUMNS, AND OBLIQUE STITCH

1–2 Pull 6 threads, leave 4, pull 6, leave 4, and pull 6. Secure the sides of the work area with a buttonhole stitch and working on the wrong side of the fabric, hemstitch the top of the work area to create bars of four threads each.

Begin hemstitching the bottom of the first pulled area by making one bar of two threads and then creating subsequent bars by grouping the remaining two threads of the first bar and two threads of the next bar. This will create a zigzag pattern. Complete the hemstitch in the entire work area.

3–4 Working on the right side of the fabric, and from right to left, pass the needle behind the fabric (upward) and then in front of the fabric downwards creating a slanted stitch; repeat to make a second stitch, coming out behind the next bar. Repeat this procedure to complete a row of double stitches across unpulled area.

5 Repeat the previous steps for remaining pulled areas.

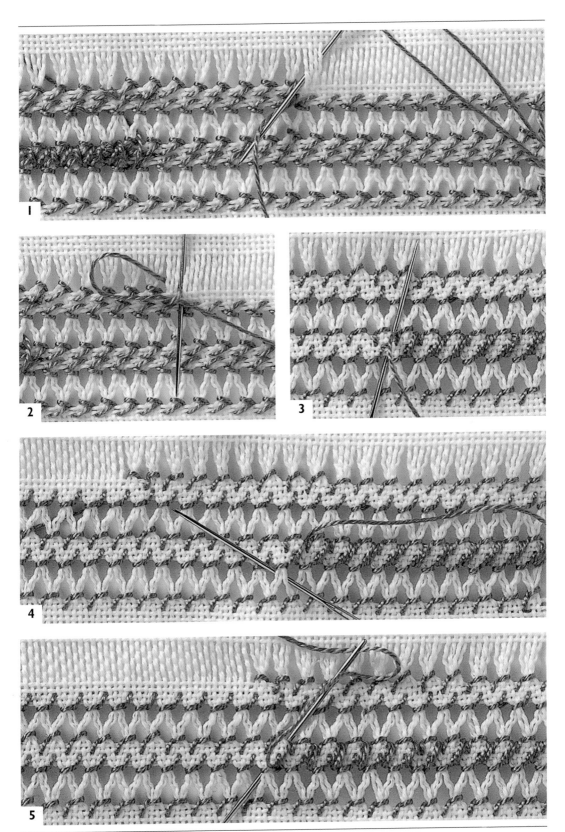

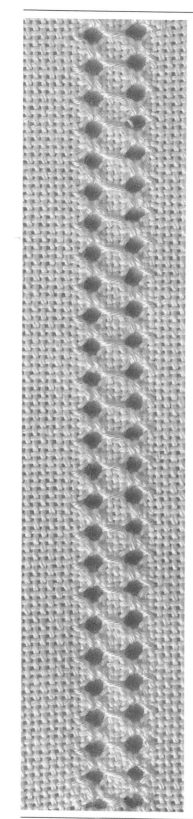

BLOCK HEMSTITCH

1 Pull 2 threads, leaving 4 threads between them. Working on the wrong side of the fabric, work hemstitch on outer edge of both bare (pulled) areas, grouping 4 threads for each bar. Using holes made by hemstitching to work a block stitch: Work a vertical stitch emerging at bottom left and inserting needle from right to left at top of next block.

2 Make a horizontal stitch across block inserting needle again at top right and bring out at bottom left, passing needle diagonally behind the fabric. Repeat this procedure.

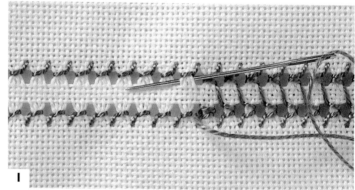

1

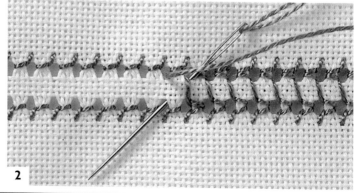

2

NET MOTIF

This motif is created on 16 threads: Pull 4 threads, leave 2, pull 4, leave 2, and pull 4.

1 Secure the ends with buttonhole stitch. Hemstitch the top bare area, making bars of 4 threads each. Working from right to left, connect these bars at the bottom and at the same time form the bars of the row below as follows: Pass the needle behind the first four threads, wrap the threads and return to the wrong side of the fabric to come out at the top of bare area below.

2 Wrap the first bar of the lower bare area and return to the top left corner to wrap the bottom of the next bar of the upper bare area. Repeat this procedure across the work area.

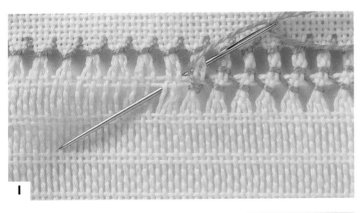

1

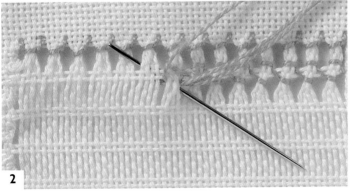

2

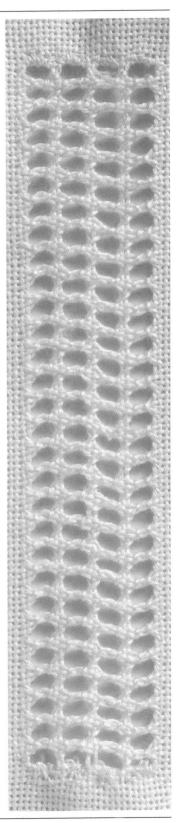

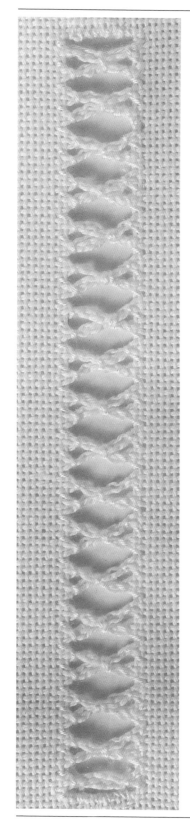

PEAHOLE HEMSTITCH

1–2 Pull 8 threads or more, depending on the type of fabric. Working hemstitch left to right, create bars of 4 threads each at top of work area.

As you work the bottom left to right, make matching bars, working over the same group of 4 threads as at the top, working as follows: Group the 4 threads with a horizontal stitch, securing it to the fabric with a small vertical stitch; repeat on next 4 threads for next bar, but omit the small vertical stitch.

3 Pass the needle behind both bars, then in front, then behind the second bar and in front of the first one, emerging at the center of the bars. Make a knot to group the bars, passing the thread up through the loop that joins the bars at the center.

4 Pass the needle down behind the group and now make the small vertical stitch to secure the stitching. Repeat these steps to complete the work area, joining pairs of bars.

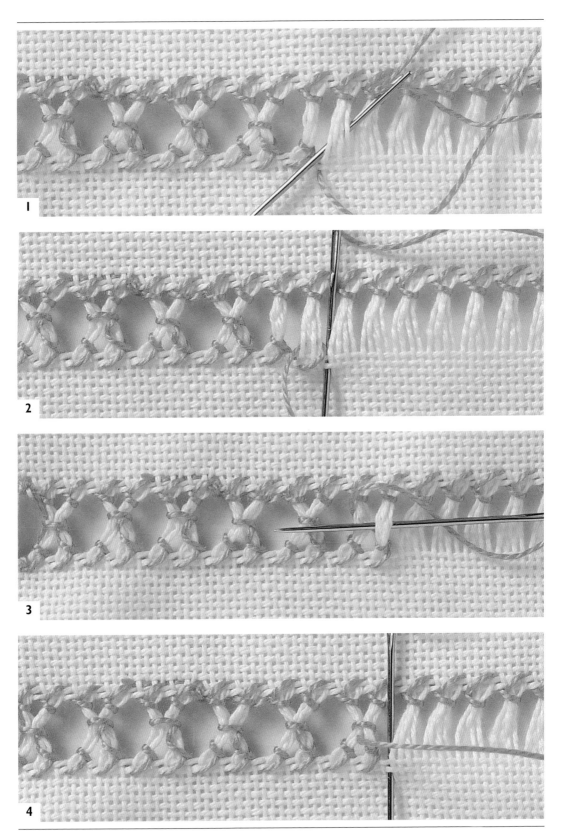

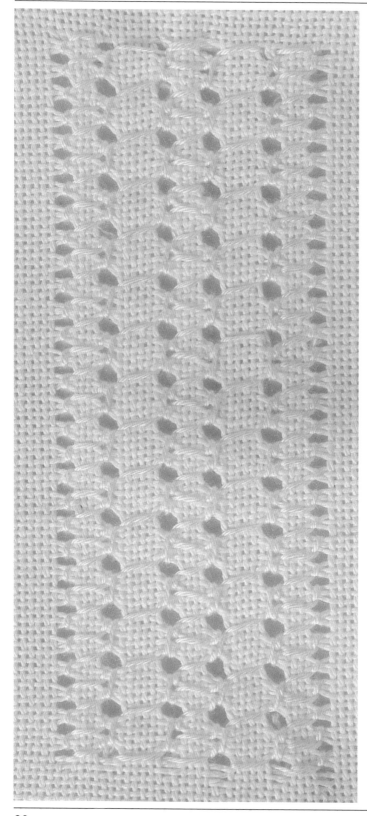

DOUBLE BLOCK STITCH

1 Work on a 36-thread area. Pull 2 threads, leave 4, pull 2, leave 6, pull 2, leave 4, pull 2, leave 6, pull 2, leave 4, and pull 2. Working from right to left, create a block stitch (see page 24) over three vertical and four horizontal threads each (shown in orange). Pass the needle behind three of the threads of the top bare area and then create a backstitch to form the first link. Passing diagonally behind the fabric, come out on the left corner of the next bare area below. Create the second link of three threads by backstitching them and then do a vertical stitch to close the block, coming out at the top left corner behind the next three threads in the fabric.

2–3–4 On the six-thread groups between, create a large block stitch (shown in blue) over six horizontal and six vertical threads. Each large block stitch equals two regular block stitches in width.

5–6 Continue alternating rows of regular block stitches with large block stitches as shown in the photograph.

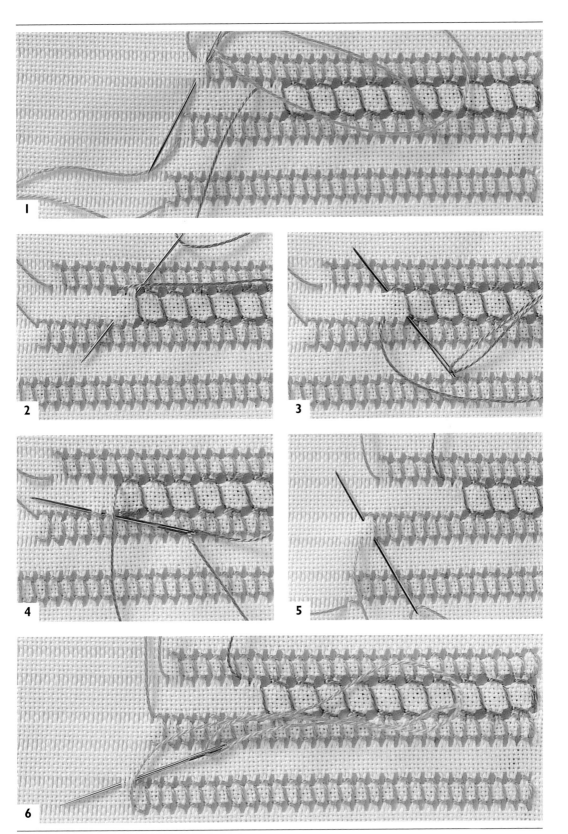

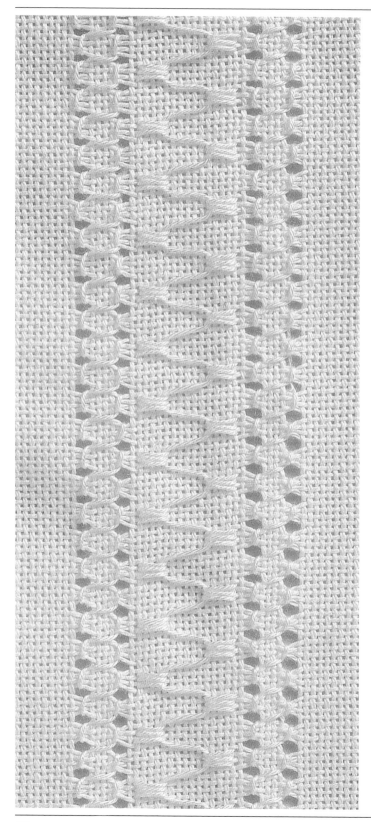

BLOCK STITCH WITH LINKED KLOSTERS

1–2 Work on a 33-thread work area. Pull 2 threads, leave 4, pull 2, leave 17, pull 2, leave 4, pull 2. Working corners in first 2 pulled (bare) areas, stitch blocks across 4 threads of 4-thread unpulled area between. In large center unpulled area, stitch 3 satin stitches for each kloster (solid motif), working stitches over 6 threads in length and leaving 1 thread unworked between blocks and klosters. Work a kloster under every other block stitch. Leaving 1 thread unworked below, work bottom row of klosters, alternating the position of the klosters.

3–4–5 Working right to left, link the klosters as shown, passing the threaded needle under the kloster stitches without catching the fabric.

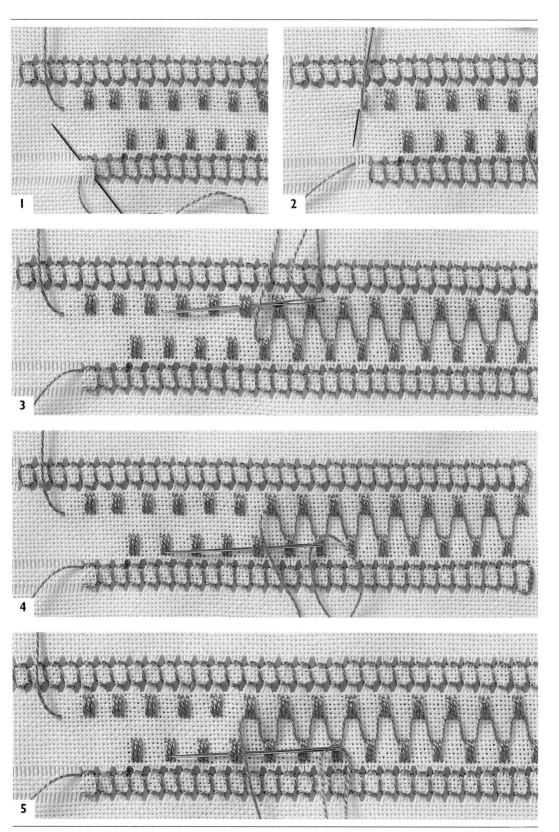

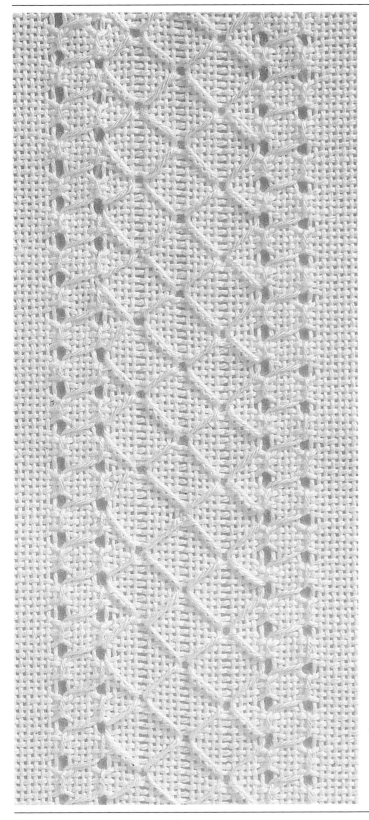

BLOCK STITCH WITH NET MOTIF

1–2 Work on 37 threads. Pull 1 and leave 5; repeat this 6 times and then pull 1 more thread. Work a block stitch row at the top and at the bottom, from right to left. Make sure the block stitches match at the top and bottom. You will have four rows in the middle, separated by 1 pulled thread.

3–4 Create one row of oblique stitches between the second and third bare areas, forming small triangles that point downward. Complete the row. Beginning on the right of the work area, work more triangles between the third and fourth bare areas to create a diamond pattern.

5–6 Repeat steps 3–4 in the remaining two rows, covering all the work area between the block stitches.

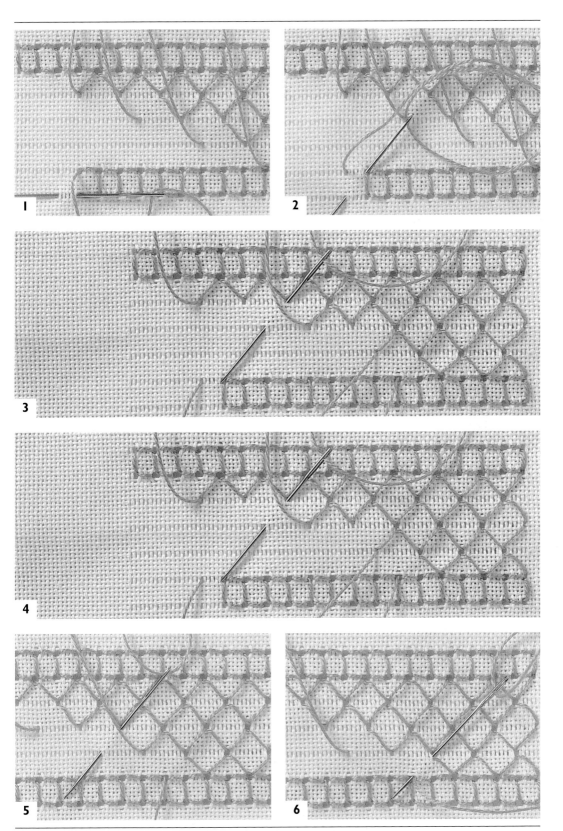

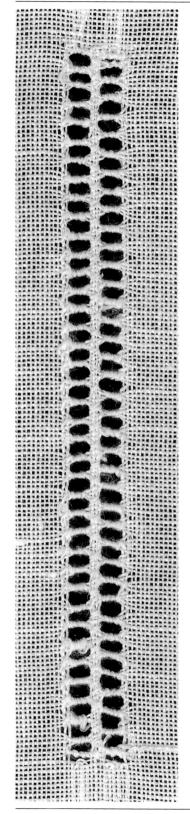

HEMSTITCH WITH ALTERNATING BARS, CORDING STITCH, AND BLOCK STITCH

I Pull 4 threads, leave 4, and pull 4. Work a row of hemstitch at top and bottom of the work area, making alternating bars of 4 threads each.

2–3–4 Work cording stitch on each bar, forming the block stitches between as you pass from upper to lower bars

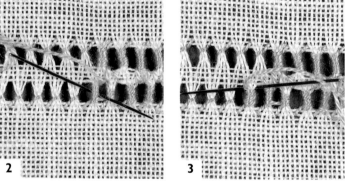

I

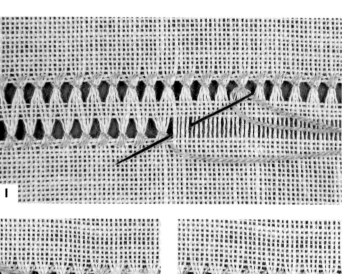

2

3

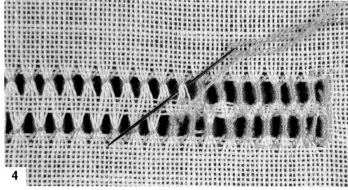

4

HEMSTITCH WITH ZIGZAG BARS

1–2–3 Pull 30 threads. Work up and down bare area as follows: Work hemstitch at top, to form 2 or 3 bars of 4 threads each. Passing thread behind bar, knot the last 2 bars together 0.5 cm below top. Continue grouping bars as in Photo 1 or 2, connecting them once at the bottom and then at the top, passing the thread along the column from one stitch to the next. If desired, work with separate threads at top and bottom.

1

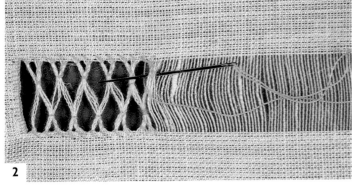

2

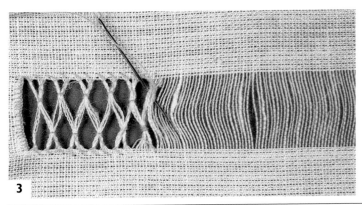

3

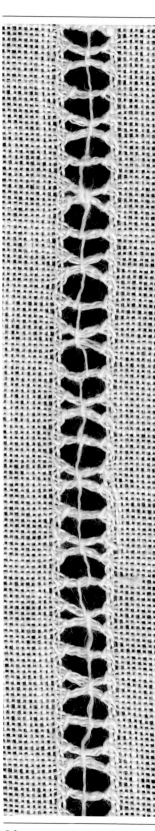

HEMSTITCH WITH LINKED BARS (KNOT STITCH)

I Pull 9 threads and secure both ends of the work area with buttonhole stitches. On the wrong side of the fabric, hemstitch the top and the bottom edges of the work area, creating bars of 4 threads each. When you finish the top row, turn the work upside down and still working on the wrong side of the fabric, do the bottom row.

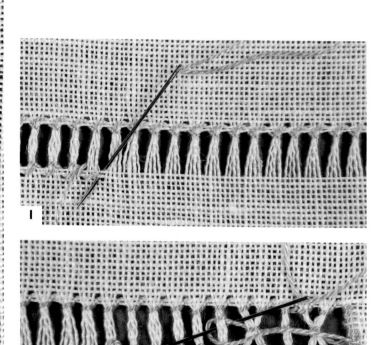

2–3   Once you have completed the top and bottom hemstitch, connect the first 2 bars with a festoon stitch, then work festoon stitch around a single bar as shown.

4   Without pulling the thread, continue to group 2 bars together with a festoon stitch, then a single bar, until you reach the end of the row. If you run out of thread and must use a new one, begin on the knot stitch of the bar, hiding it under the threads of the bar.

VARIATION—HEMSTITCH WITH 3 LINKED BARS

In this motif, you can group 3 or more bars with a festoon stitch, creating a small design. We recommend working on the wrong side of the fabric, because it will be easier to move from one group to the next without showing the knots.

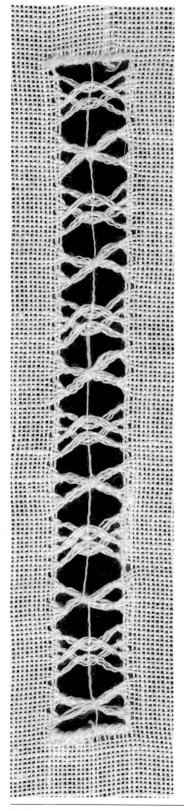

ALTERNATING LINKED BARS

I Pull 19 threads. Secure the ends with buttonhole stitch. Hemstitch the top and bottom of the work area, creating bars of 3 threads each and working on the wrong side of the fabric. Now work from right to left, beginning in the center of the buttonhole stitch end. Create a knot stitch to group two bars.

2 To group 4 intertwined bars, use needle to catch third bar and pull it to the right, pass needle under the third bar and over first bar, catch fourth bar and pull it to the right, pass needle under fourth bar and over second bar, ending at left of completed motif.

3 Alternating knotted pairs of bars with groups of 4 intertwined bars, complete working across bare area.

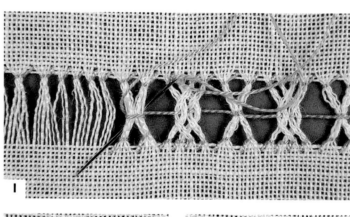

I

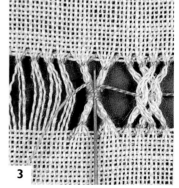

2

3

HEMSTITCH WITH UPSIDE-DOWN BARS

I Pull 12 threads and secure the ends of the work area with buttonhole stitch. Work across top edge, creating bars of 8 threads each, working as follows: Work hemstitch, creating first 8-thread bar, pass needle along top edge behind next 2 threads, in front of next 4 threads, then behind last 2 threads of next bar; repeat across, alternating grouped and ungrouped threads. Secure thread end.

2–3 Turn fabric upside down and repeat the process, alternating, so grouped threads at one edge are ungrouped at opposite edge, and vice versa.

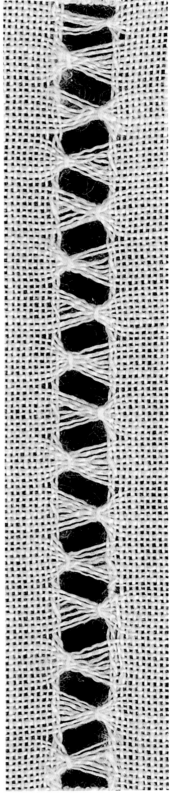

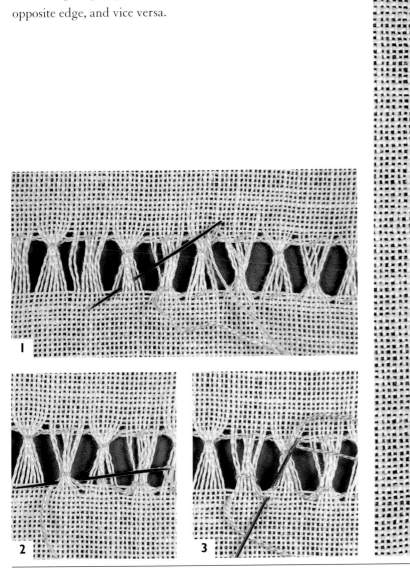

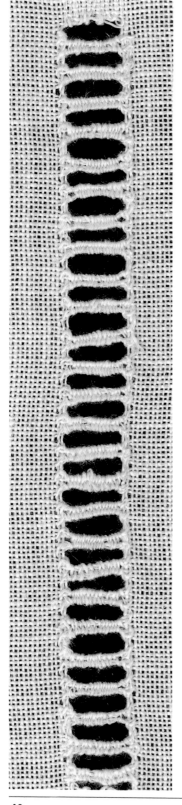

DARNING STITCH BARS

1 Pull 14 threads for the height of the work area. Work a row of hemstitches at the top and one at the bottom, creating bars of 3 threads each, that match at the top and the bottom. Work on the wrong side of the fabric, from left to right.

2 The darning stitch connects the bars two by two. Begin at the right end of the work area, working on the right side of the work. Pass the needle under one bar and over the next.

3 Working in the opposite direction, pass the needle under first, then over next bar. Continue working up the pair of bars, alternating the direction of the needle with each stitch, weaving in and out as before. Repeat with each pair of bars, working up one pair and down the next.

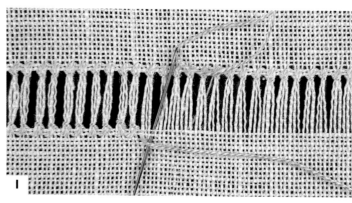

1

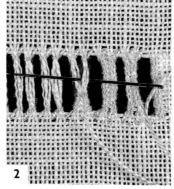

2

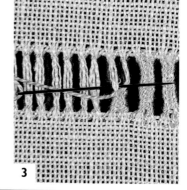

3

HEMSTITCH WITH FESTOONED BARS

1 Pull 8 threads. Hemstitch top and bottom of the 2-thread work area. Beginning on the first bar, do one festoon (buttonhole) stitch.

2–3 Work each new festoon stitch, adding one bar until you have a group of four. The bars are lined together in the center. Continue by reversing the procedure, omitting one bar each festoon stitch until only one bar is left.

4 Once you have completed the first motif, pass the thread to the wrong side of the fabric under the openwork stitch. Come out on the right side of the work in the next spot to begin a new group of bars working up one group and down the next.

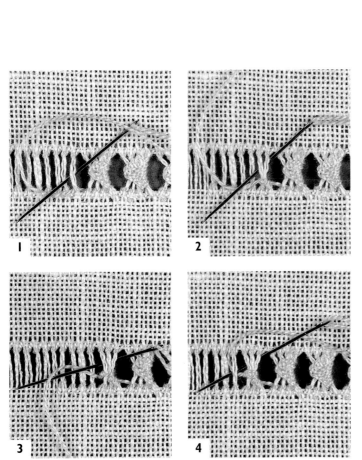

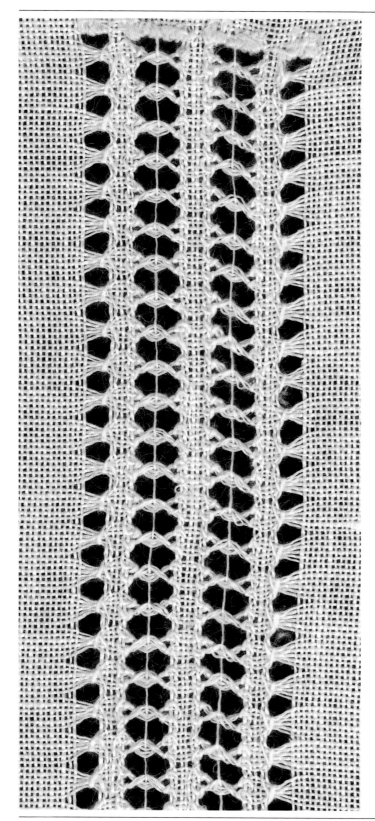

DOUBLE HEMSTITCH AND LINKED BARS

1–2 Pull 5 threads, leave 5, pull 9, leave 6, pull 9, leave 5, pull 4. On the wrong side of the fabric, at the base of the first bare area, work one row of hemstitch, making bars of 6 threads each and stitching under 2 threads to secure each stitch. Hemstitch the edges of the two larger bare areas at the center of the work area, working from the wrong side and securing the thread at each end of the work area on each row.

3–4–5 Now working on the right side of fabric, link bars in each section as follows: Secure the thread at the center of the end of work area, then pass the needle under the second bar, catching it and drawing it to the right (3), then over the first bar to interlink them (4); repeat on each pair of bars across, securing thread at end of work area. Work hemstitch along top of lower bare area to complete border.

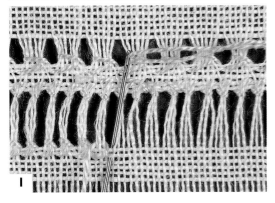

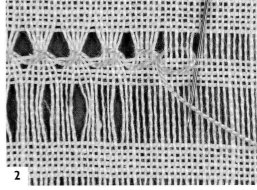

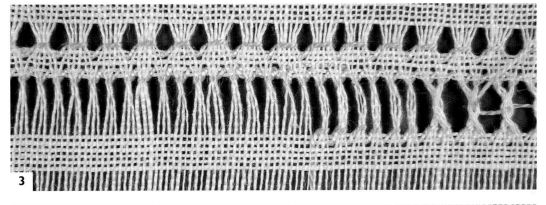

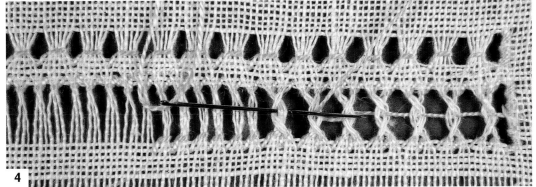

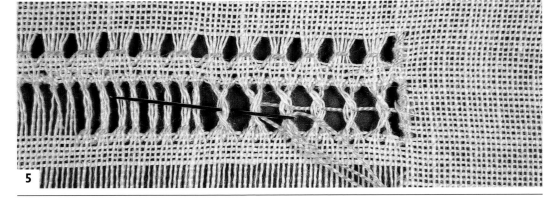

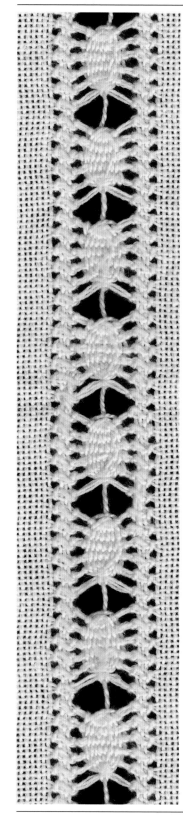

HEMSTITCH WITH FAN MOTIF

1–2–3 Pull 1 thread, leave 4, pull 18, leave 4, and pull 1. Complete two rows of block stitches above and below the pulled area, grouping 3 threads for each bar.

4 Secure the thread at the center of the end of the bare area and begin the pattern, working on 6 bars at a time.

5 Weave the needle over and under the bars two or three times, working out from the center and skipping the first bar, the anchoring bar for this motif.

6 Once you have completed the previous step, create a border for the work area with chain stitches to secure the pattern. Then, pass the needle to the wrong side of the fabric and come out on the tip of the fan shape to begin a new fan on the next group of bars.

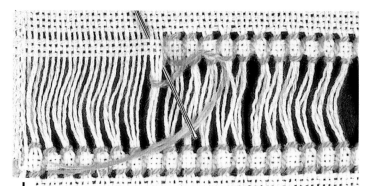

1

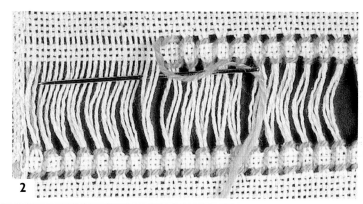

2

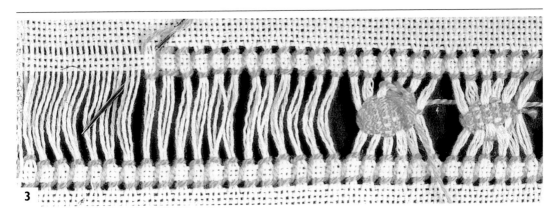

3

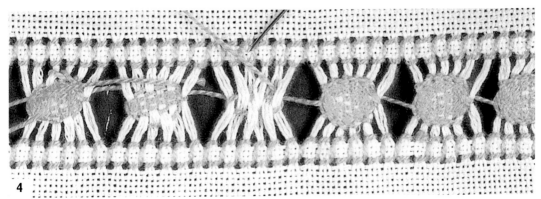

4

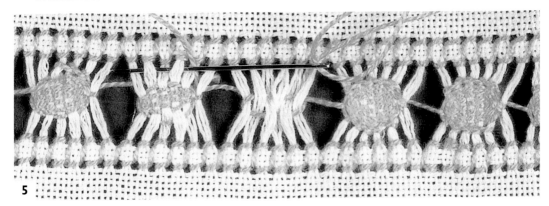

5

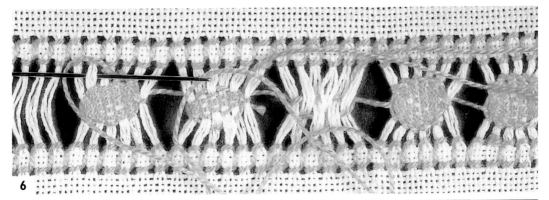

6

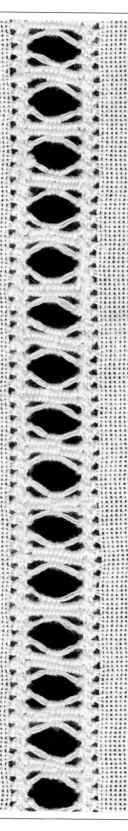

DARNING STITCH WITH A SPIDER MOTIF

I Pull 1 thread, leave 4, pull 12, leave 4, and pull 1. Work two rows of block stitch, forming matching bars of 3 threads each.

2–3 Work on 4 bars to create the motif. On center 2 bars, work a darning stitch once from the right, once from the left, for one third of the height of the bars.

4 Now work on all 4 bars in one group, by creating 6 darning stitches, passing over and under the threads.

5–6 Now work only on the center bars for the remaining length until you reach the block stitch. Pass the thread behind the block stitch and come out in the block stitch at the center of the next group of bars, to begin another motif. Alternate working up one group and down the next.

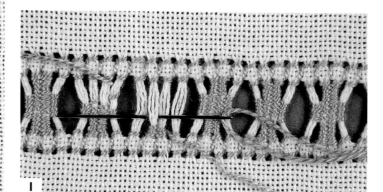

I

2

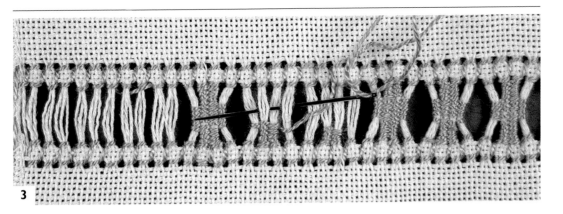

3

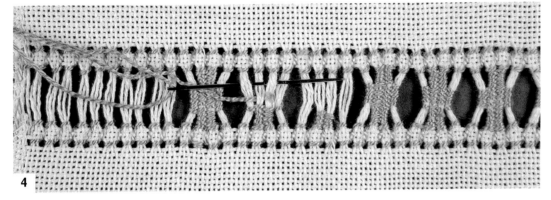

4

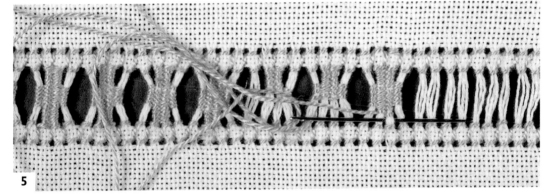

5

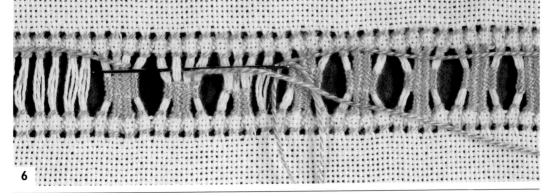

6

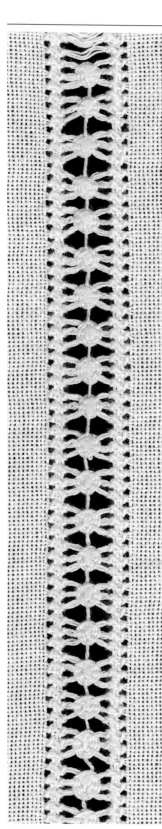

HEMSTITCH WITH BLOCK STITCH AND KNOT MOTIF

1   Pull 1 thread, leave 3, pull 18, leave 3, pull 1. Work a top and bottom row of block stitch, forming matching bars of 3 threads. You are now ready to begin the motif in the center of the work area. Group 3 bars together for each motif by wrapping the thread around the 3 bars, secure the thread and come out on the right side of the work.

2–3   Work around the 3 grouped bars with a darning stitch 4 or 5 times, forming a small circle. Repeat this procedure across.

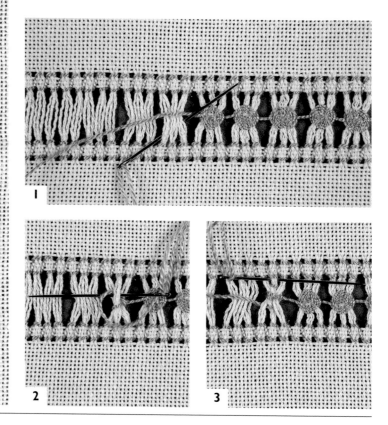

SMALL FESTOON HEMSTITCH

1 Pull 18 threads. Hemstitch the top and bottom edges, forming bars of 5 threads each. Working on the right side of the fabric, group 3 bars with a festoon (buttonhole) stitch.

2 Work 5 to 8 festoon stitches until you get near the end of the bars.

3 Pass thread through the last stitch and join the next 3 bars to repeat the procedure.

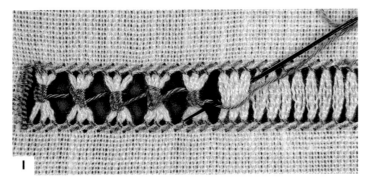

1

2

3

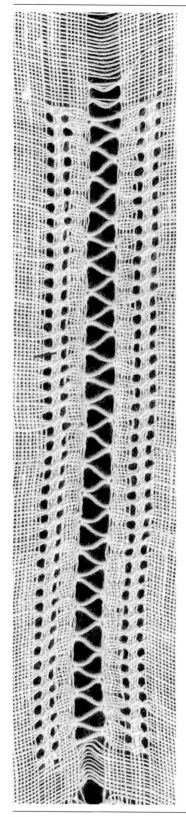

HEMSTITCH WITH ALTERNATING BARS

1–2   Pull 1 thread, leave 4, pull 1, leave 6, pull 7, leave 6, pull 1, leave 4, and pull 1 on right side, work 2 rows of block stitching on the top and bottom edges of the work area, over 4 threads on the right side of the fabric. Then, working on the wrong side of the fabric, hemstitch the top and bottom of the central bare area, forming bars of 4 threads.

3   Wrap the first bar from top to bottom with a cording stitch, beginning on the left, and make a small stitch at the base to secure it.

4   Join this bar to the next one, connecting them at the base. Cord the new bar coming out at the top to connect another bar, and return with a cording stitch to the bottom of the new bar, creating a zigzag pattern.

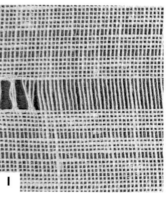

1

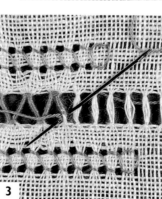

2

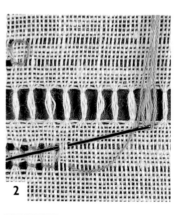

3

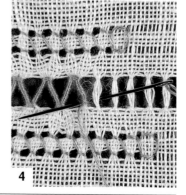

4

LADDER HEMSTITCH

I Pull 18 threads. Hemstitch the top and bottom edges of the bare area, forming bars of 4 threads each. Join the first and second bar with a darning stitch until you have covered one-third of the height of the bars.

2–3 Shift, omitting the first bar and continue on second and third bars with a darning stitch for 7 or 8 stitches. Shift to continue darning the third and fourth bars. Pass the thread on the wrong side of the fabric to new group of bars. Darn 4 bars together for one-third of the height, then shift, omitting 1 bar and adding next bar and darn the center of the work. Shift again to connect the last bars with a darning stitch. Work 1 group of bars up and the next down. Alternate 2-bar and 4-bar groups, covering the unworked sections of the bars partially worked for the previous group. Pass the thread along the wrong side of the fabric to start the next group. You do not need to make knots to secure the thread; it will be secured by the darning stitches.

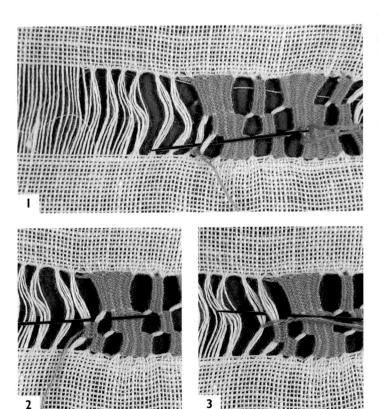

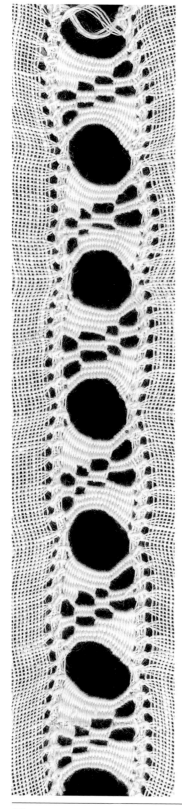

PINE CONE HEMSTITCH

I　Pull 1 thread, leave 4, pull 20, leave 4, and pull 1. Do 2 rows of block stitch on the edges of the bare area to form matching bars of 4 threads each. Connect the bars, darning over and under first 5 bars, about 0.5 cm of the height of the bars.

2–3　Continue by omitting 1 bar and working on the other 4 with darning stitch covering 0.5 cm. in height each time. Omit 1 bar and work the other 3 bars (always with a darning stitch), covering 0.5 cm. Then omit 1 and do a darning stitch on the other 2 bars until you reach the block stitch on the edge of the bar area. Work this same motive from the opposite side, forming an opening between (2 pine cone patterns made). Next to these, darn 2 bars together, shifting to work over bare sections of bars left by previous motifs. Continue across with the 2 pine cone motifs in opposite directions alternated with the 2-bar group, working so all bare sections of the bars are covered.

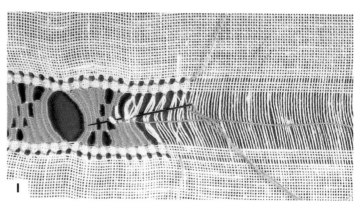

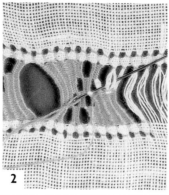

I

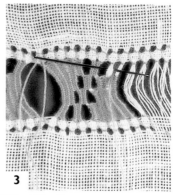

2　　　　　　　**3**

PYRAMID HEMSTITCH

I Pull 1 thread, leave 4, pull 3, leave 4, and pull 1. Work block stitch over 4 threads along both edges of the bare area. For this motif, you may find it useful to use a hoop in order to keep the threads closer together while you are working on this pattern.

2–3 Starting on 2 bars for the pyramid, work a darning stitch for 1 cm. Adding a new bar to each side, continue darning on 4 bars for 0.5 cm more, then on 6 bars for 0.5 cm, then on 8 bars to edge. Skip 8 bars after the top of completed pyramid and work a new pyramid, starting on next 2 bars. (Two unworked bars remain between the motifs at the bottom.) Repeat across row. Then working on unused sections at top of pyramid bars, work darning stitch over 2 bars, shifting over to a new bar as you cover each section of bar closest to the pyramid. Fill in the areas between the pyramids and the first 2-bar motif, working darning stitch over 2 bars on unused sections of the bars as shown.

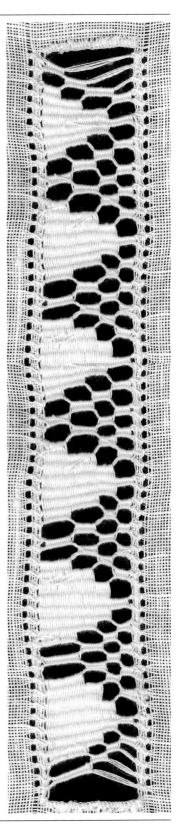

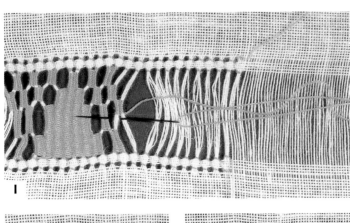

1

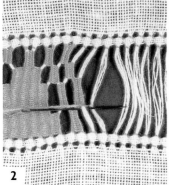

2

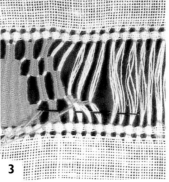

3

HEMSTITCH WITH COLUMNS

I Pull 20 threads. On wrong side of fabric, form bars of 4 threads each, hemstitching at top and bottom. On right side of fabric, connect 2 bars with darning stitch to form a column and, at midpoint, take 2 threads of adjacent unworked bar at right, then of the unworked bar at left, joining each to column for 1 stitch (for diamond motif). Continue darning just original 2 bars to end of column.

2–3–4 Pass needle under the hemstitch, skipping next (diamond) bar. Work following 2 bars with darning stitch for new column. At center, connect remaining 2 threads of skipped bar and 2 threads of next bar on other side as before; then complete column on 2 bars to edge. Working 1 motif up, then 1 down, make 2-bar columns across, with a diamond between.

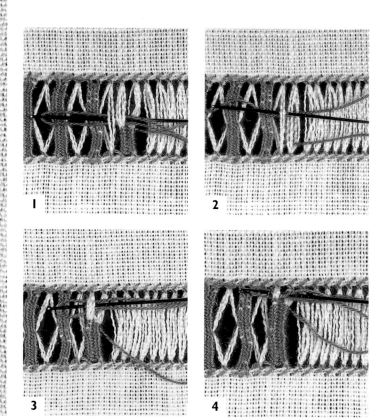

SPIDER HEMSTITCH

1–2–3 Pull 22 threads. Hemstitch edges, making bars of 4 threads each. At the center of the bare area, with a new thread, connect 4 bars with a chain stitch. Pass under and over the bars with a darning stitch 3 times. Pointing the needle towards the wrong side at the center of the "spider," pick the linking thread and work a few buttonhole stitches, and then return to the new group of bars and continue with darning stitches.

1

2

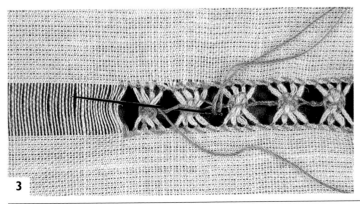

3

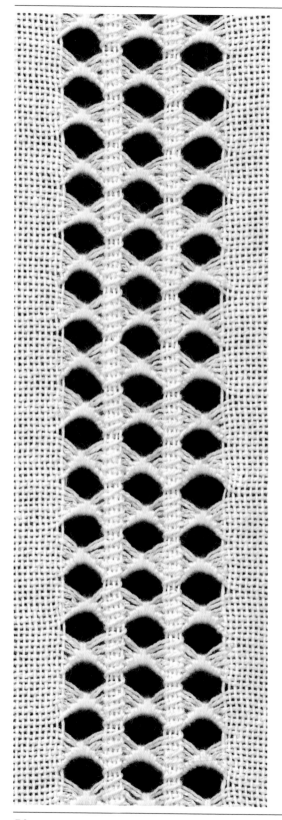

FESTOON HEMSTITCH

1–2 Pull 7 threads, leave 4, pull 7, leave 4, and pull 7. Going from right to left, make 2 rows of half block stitches on the unpulled threads left between bare areas to form bars of 2 threads.

3–4 Starting in the bottom bare area, working from left, wrap 1 bar (2 threads) with 2 cording stitches. Add another bar and wrap with 2 more stitches, then add third, then at the midpoint, the fourth bar, working 2 cording stitches each time. Now reverse this pattern, working 2 cording stitches and omitting 1 bar each time until you reach the edge with a single bar.

At the end of a group, pass through the center of the block stitch, above, on the wrong side of the work, and repeat the process in the bare area above, grouping bars to make a new motif. Work up and down the bare areas working motifs, or, if you prefer, just work across 1 row at a time, working up 1 motif and down the next.

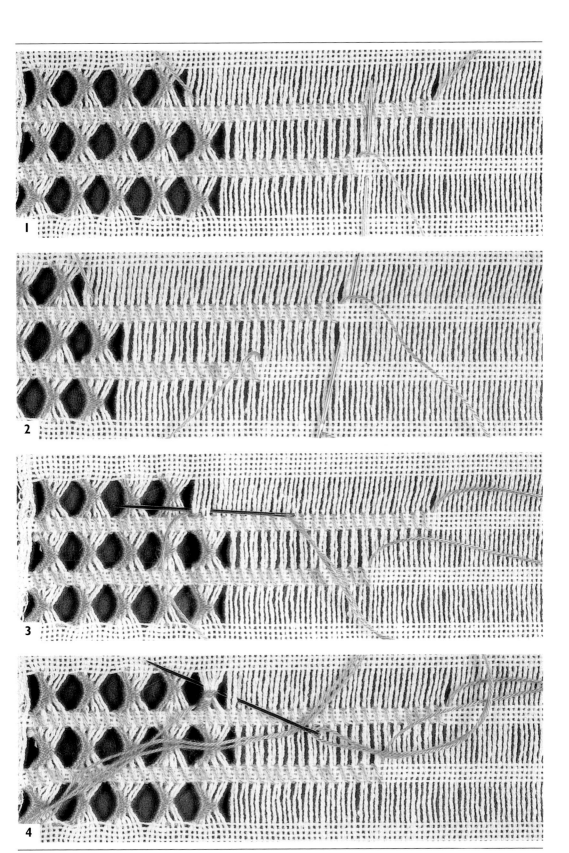

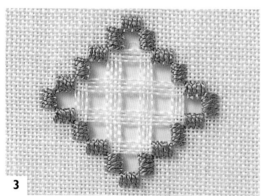

TRADITIONAL HARDANGER

1 Omit making a knot to begin. Instead, leave a bit of thread and secure it to the fabric with a backstitch. Once the embroidery is completed, pass the leftover thread to the wrong side of the work and cut it. Repeat this procedure with all leftover threads. The easiest way to divide the fabric and count the thread is to embroider 5 satin stitches together, each worked over 4 threads. To continue in a straight line, remember that the exit point of the last stitch in a row is the exit point of the first stitch of the next row. Keep the thread up close to the previous stitch while you work. To make diagonal kloster blocks, follow these procedures, changing the directions of the rows.

2 To create a square or a diamond, work in a straight line. You can use 1 row of stitches as the link between 2 shapes.

3 After you complete the border of the motif with the satin stitches, securing the edges, you will be ready to pull the threads. Cut only the threads that are secured on the edges. Do not cut threads that have not been secured by the satin stitches. Cut the threads very close to the satin stitches, as shown in the picture. Use tweezers to pull the threads more easily. Once completed, your square or diamond will have a net pattern.

4 *Wrapped bars*. Wrap the threads left inside the square or diamond with a cording stitch, wrapping around a group of threads many times with the needle. To achieve an even motif, be sure to wrap each bar with the same number of loops. Use pearl cotton thread for a more delicate effect or cotton thread for embroidery to do the wrapped bars. Many Hardanger projects will indicate which type of thread to use for this stitch.

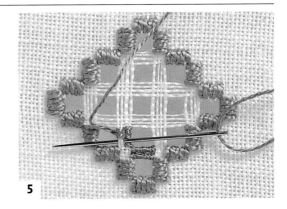

5 **_Double wrapped bars_**. This is a more elegant variety of the previous stitch, although it is not more difficult. Divide each group of threads into 2 groups, and wrap each half separately.

5

6 **_Woven bars_**. Work a darning stitch, bringing the needle out in the middle of the group of threads and alternate wrapping loops around each half of the group.

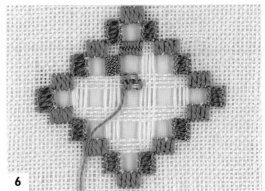

6

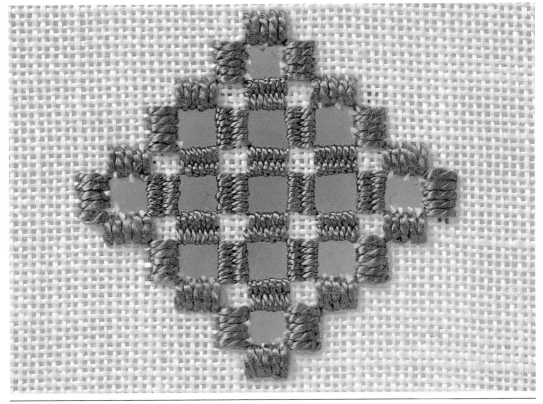

I *Woven bars with loops.* Do a woven bar and leave a small loop on the outside. Pass the needle through the loop and pull the thread. Repeat the procedure for each woven bar.

2–3 The empty squares made by pulling the threads are finished with floating stitches, usually called dove's eye stitches, that give a touch of elegance to the work. Work from left to right in a large festoon stitching pattern. Anchor the thread in the center of the small kloster square at edge. Working around the edge of the square, go to the next side, passing the needle under the center stitch. Continue around each side to complete the pattern. Dove's eye stitches are very decorative. Even one dove's eye stitch in the center of a square or a diamond is an elegant detail in a project.

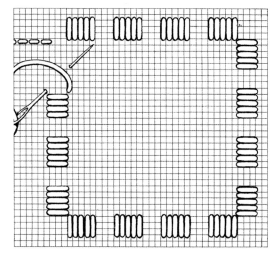

SATIN STITCH

The first step in Hardanger embroidery is to do the border of the motif by using satin stitches to form kloster blocks. This stitch covers 4 threads and the distance between stitches is 1 thread. Therefore, there are 4 threads left for every 5 stitches. To create straight corners with the satin stitch border, skip 4 threads of the fabric; to create oblique borders (a diamond), alternate a group of satin stitches on 4 threads of the fabric with one group on 4 warp threads.

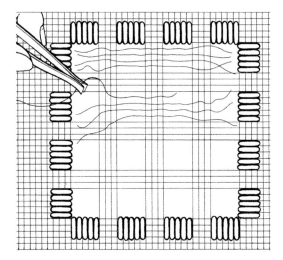

HOW TO PULL THE THREAD

After you complete the border of the motif with the satin stitches, securing the edges, you will be ready to pull the threads. Cut only the threads that are secured on the edges. Do not cut threads that have not been secured by the satin stitches. Cut the threads very close to the satin stitches, as shown in the picture. Use tweezers to pull the threads more easily. Once completed, your square or diamond will have a net pattern.

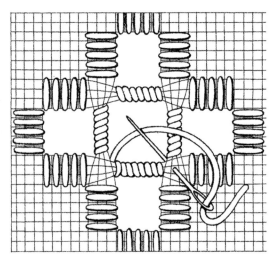

DOVE'S EYE STITCH

This stitch is done in a small square made with corded or woven bar stitching. Pass the needle in the center of the corner of the square, making a loop. Repeat this procedure 3 more times, always ensuring that you pass the needle through the loop. After you complete this in all four sides of the square, return to your starting point and secure the thread.

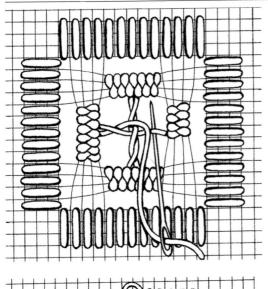

VERTICAL AND HORIZONTAL FILLING STITCH

On a small square made by woven (darned) bar stitching, pass the needle through the center of the bottom side, then go through the center of the opposite side, leaving the passed thread a little loose. Then pass the needle to the wrong side of the work and wrap the thread once over the passed thread, returning to your starting point. Secure the thread. On the wrong side of the work, pass the needle under the woven bar stitches to reach the center of the adjacent side of the square. Pull the needle to the right side of the work and repeat the procedure to form another passed thread that crosses the first one horizontally. Wrap this passed thread and then secure the thread on the wrong side of the work.

DIAGONAL FILLING STITCH

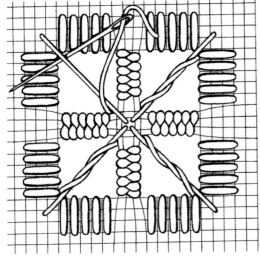

After you complete all the darned bar stitches, make the first diagonal stitch starting at one corner and stitching into center crossed threads, then on the opposite corner. Wrapping thread loosely around diagonal stitches just made and passing thread under the center, return to original corner. Repeat process to make diagonal stitches on remaining 2 corners.

MALTESE CROSS

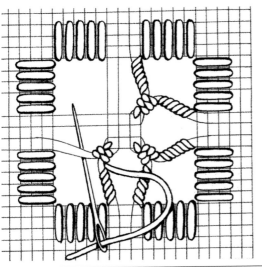

At one corner, wrap 2 vertical threads with a cording stitch, working halfway to center square of unpulled threads. Now begin working darning stitch on same 2 threads and the next 2 horizontal threads at the corner until you reach the corner. Pass the needle under the darning stitches to reach the unworked half of the horizontal threads; wrap them with cording stitch back to edge of square. Repeat at each corner.

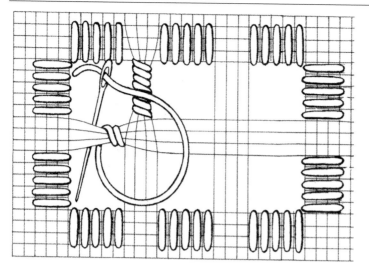

WRAPPED BARS (CORDING STITCH)

Wrap the threads with a cording stitch. The easiest method is to wrap tightly the 4 remaining threads at once, passing from one group to the next and using the same number of wrapping stitches.

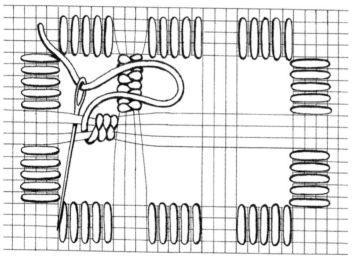

WOVEN BARS (DARNING STITCH)

This is a very popular Hardanger stitch. To do woven bars, pass the needle over 2 threads and under the other 2 threads in the kloster block, weaving back and forth on each group of 4 threads until they are completely covered by the stitch. Make sure the stitches are very close together.

STITCH SYMBOLS

Satin stitch

Festoon stitch

Satin star stitch

Cording stitch on groups
of 4 threads

Cording stitch on
groups of 2 threads
or double bars

Darning stitch

Darning stitch bars
with loops

Diagonal dove's
eye stitch

Straight dove's
eye stitch

Ideas and Projects

Linen Place Mats

These linen place mats are an elegant touch for any breakfast table, or a tea or coffee tray. They are an impeccable alternative to a traditional tablecloth.

Cut a 50 x 45 cm linen rectangle and make a 2-cm border. Hemstitch all around the rectangle, making sure the stitches go through the back of the 2-cm border. Use #80 thread for the openwork stitch and #25 thread for the darning stitch.

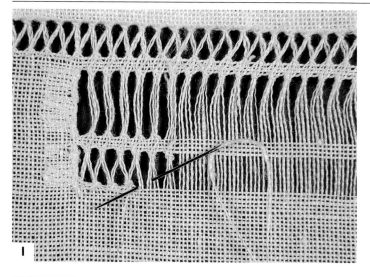

1

I Make a 2-cm border all around place mat, basting the corners to be pulled later. On each edge, pull 8 threads, then on both sides of one corner, leave 4, pull 20, leave 4, pull 8 more. Repeat on opposite corner. Secure threads at the ends of work areas. Hemstitch the first area pulled all around the mat, grouping 4 threads per stitch. For zigzag pattern, divide each bar in half and take 2 threads from 1 bar and 2 from the next bar. Then on inner areas (at 2 opposite corners), work half-block stitches across 4 remaining threads bordering 20-thread pulled area, making matching bars of 4 threads each. Work zigzag pattern on inner bare area.

2–3–4 At the corners, work a cording stitch over the length of each group of unpulled threads. Fill in the corner squares as follows: Draw thread across center square from side to side and

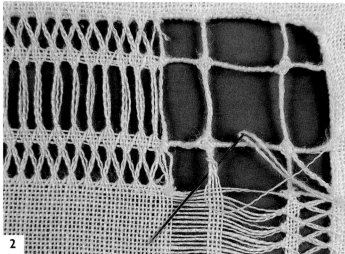

3

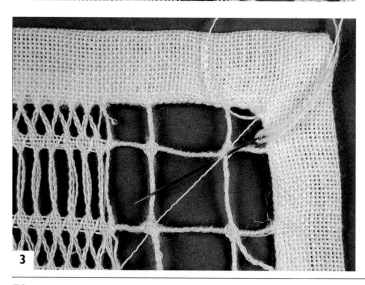

2

corner to corner to form a star motif, and from corner to corner on small corner squares. Wrap the threads with a cording stitch. Pass the thread in a tight spiral around the intersections of the pulled and corded threads.

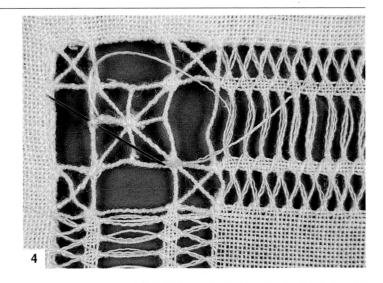

4

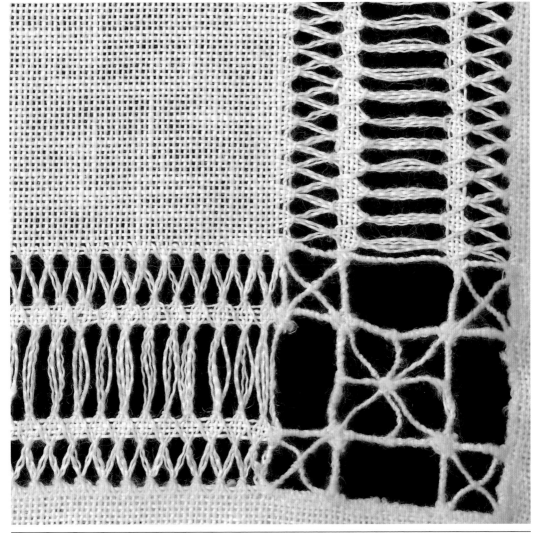

Place Mat and Napkin in Emiane Fabric

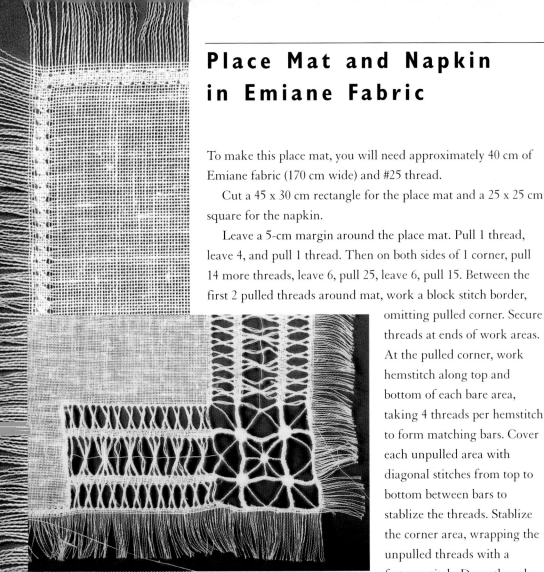

To make this place mat, you will need approximately 40 cm of Emiane fabric (170 cm wide) and #25 thread.

Cut a 45 x 30 cm rectangle for the place mat and a 25 x 25 cm square for the napkin.

Leave a 5-cm margin around the place mat. Pull 1 thread, leave 4, and pull 1 thread. Then on both sides of 1 corner, pull 14 more threads, leave 6, pull 25, leave 6, pull 15. Between the first 2 pulled threads around mat, work a block stitch border, omitting pulled corner. Secure threads at ends of work areas. At the pulled corner, work hemstitch along top and bottom of each bare area, taking 4 threads per hemstitch to form matching bars. Cover each unpulled area with diagonal stitches from top to bottom between bars to stablize the threads. Stablize the corner area, wrapping the unpulled threads with a festoon stitch. Draw threads diagonally across the small squares as shown, making a star stitch in the center square, then work darning stitch spirals at intersections and center of star stitch. On the center row of bars, work a linked column pattern, grouping 3 bars, then 1 bar alternately, wrapping each group or single bar once at center. Above and below link row, group 2 bars together across row, concealing thread in bars to edge as you move between groups. Pull threads to fringe outer edges of mat.

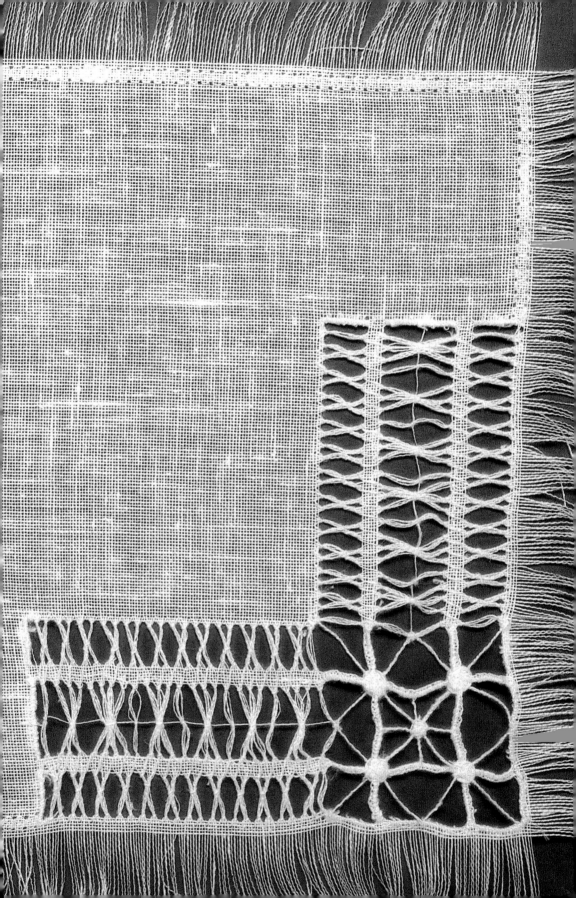

Beautiful Place Mat

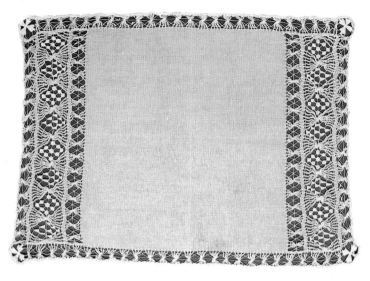

Leaving 5 threads at edge, pull threads for 2.5-cm-wide area all around for border. At each end of mat, leave 7 threads at long and short edges to separate border, pull 6-cm-wide area, leave 7 threads as before, pull 2-cm-wide area. You may find it useful to use a hoop for this project.

On 7-thread borders, work a double knot (herringbone) stitch along edges, making matching bars of 5 threads each. In outer pulled area, group 4 bars at center with a knot stitch, adjusting number as needed at corners. With separate thread, link each bar at top of first group, pass needle under knot of next bar, pass needle under edge stitching (between groups),

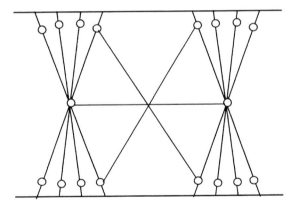

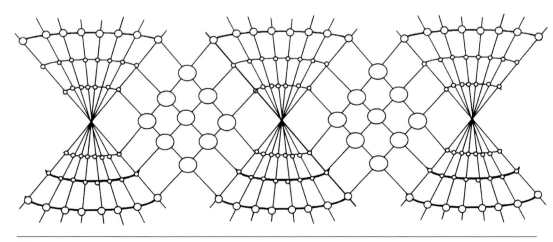

then under knot of next group; repeat, weaving edge to edge, working to corner. With new thread, work in same manner again, working in the tops and edges skipped by previous thread. Form cross motif at corners working darning stitch over linking threads.

Work wide bare area, grouping 8 bars at center with knot stitch. With separate thread, link each bar across top (a bit below top), then on next group link each bar (below center), then at top of next group, and so on across, working up and down. Work 2 more new threads in same way, but always a bit below the previous thread. Work 3 more threads over skipped areas. Where threads intersect between bar groups, work a darning stitch spiral over each intersection. Repeat at other end of mat.

Repeat outer border pattern across remaining inner bare area and each end of mat. Work darning or festoon stitch around outer edge of mat to stabilize it.

Elegant Doily

For each square, pull 16 horizontal threads, leave 8, pull 16, leave 8, pull 16. Then repeat with vertical threads over same area to form a square. Stitch the edges with a festoon (buttonhole) stitch worked toward the center of the work, securing thread ends under the stitching.

On each unpulled 8-thread row, make 2 bars, working each bar with darning stitch over 4 threads. Work bars from outer edge to intersections of unpulled threads and between intersections (around center square).

In the center of each of the 9 small squares, work a dove's eye as follows: Secure the thread at the center on one side, make a long stitch across corner to next side, stitch in center of this side and cross thread over the previous stitch to form a small loop, stitch across corner to next side, and continue around, always crossing thread to form the small loop on each side. Return to starting point, loop over original thread and secure thread. *Note:* The outer edge of this place mat is finished with a turned-under border and a crocheted edging.

Border Design with Diamond Motif

Pull 1 thread, leave 4, pull 30, leave 4, pull 1. Work oblique stitches over unpulled 4 threads at top and bottom of work area, slanting stitches from top-left to right-bottom and making matching bars of 4 threads each. Group 8 bars, working left to right as follows: Working 6 darning stitches for each joining, starting at center of bars, join first 2 bars. Working upward, omit first bar and join second bar to next bar for 6 stitches. Shifting with each joining, work until center 2 bars are joined at top, then shifting downward, work to center right edge of 8-bar group. Working down, then up, complete lower half to correspond to top. Join bars within the same manner, working inward to center of motif. Repeat across row.

VARIATION OF THE DIAMOND PATTERN

Do a simple hemstitch at the top and at the bottom of a fairly wide work area. Connect groups of eight. Beginning at the bottom, work left to right with a cording stitch for six passes connecting the fourth and fifth bars. Then add the third and the sixth and work six more passes with the same stitching. Then add the second and the seventh bars and work on all the bars for six more passes. Add the first and the eighth bars for six passes and then omit the first and the eighth bars and work on the remaining bars for six more passes. Gradually omit two bars at a time until you are left with the two central bars that are connected at the top. Pass the thread to the stitch where you will begin the next group.

Nightshirt with Festooned Neckline

Add a touch of elegance to one of those
nightshirts found in your grandmother's trunk
with a festooned neckline (directions on pages
56–57). Transform it into a summer outfit by
adding a decorative sash to it.

Using contrasting threads in this thick
weave linen shirt will highlight your
Hardanger embroidery.

Curtains with a Peahole Stitch Motif

These curtains will look beautiful in your home and make an excellent gift. Use 100% linen fabric and work with hemstitches and peahole stitches.

The delicate flat stitches on the ends of the pulled threads secure the work and make it easier to continue with the embroidery.

Use #25 thread for the openwork stitch and a mouliné thread for the embroidery.

Candy Sachets

These cheerful candy bags are great stocking
stuffers or gifts for a birthday or other special
events.

Cut a 12 x 35 cm piece of linen. Make a 2-cm
border at the top of the fabric. Hem the border.
Pull 10 threads below the border; from the wrong
side of the fabric, hemstitch the edges of the work
area, making matching bars of 3 threads each all
across piece. You can also decorate the center of
the sachet by pulling threads and creating
different Hardanger patterns using blocks, zigzag,
alternating bars, and other patterns you have just
learned in this book.

Fold fabric with right sides together; sew sides
and bottom to form a pouch. Turn right side out.

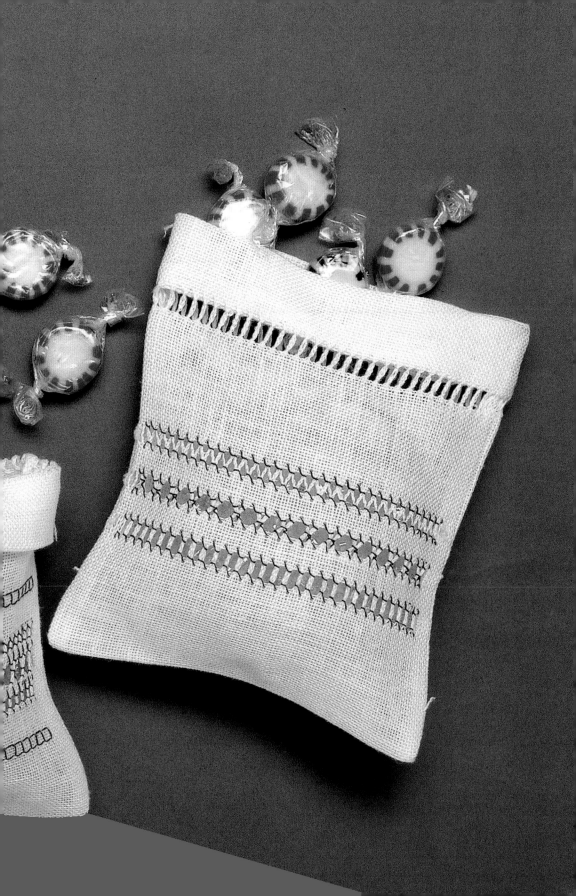

Elegant Tablecloth

Cut a 140 x 140 cm square of linen. Make a
2-cm border. Define center area, pulling
threads for peahole hemstitch border (pages
26–27); work a star stitch at each corner.

For inner border, cut triangles from lace
fabric; sew them in place, cutting away
underlying linen. Secure cut edges by working
darning stitch through both layers.

Between corners, pull 2 or 3 threads along
each side and hemstitch edges making bars of
3 threads wrapped with cording stitch.

Accent for Sheets

One of the most important types of stitching in this kind of embroidery is the darning stitch. It is a beautiful type of stitching that will allow you to create very decorative patterns. Projects embroidered with darning stitching patterns will be more resilient, especially in those cases where the pattern requires pulling out large numbers of threads. The most simple pattern you can create by darning stitching is a row of bars. The number of threads to pull out will vary depending on the pattern. If you work on an even number of pulled threads and from the center of the work area, you will be able to create alternating bars. In order to go from one group of bars to the next, pass the needle under the stitching of the group of bars already formed. Darning stitching can be created on three or four groups of threads and will allow for countless variations of different patterns.

In order not to damage the fabric, always use blunt needles when working on a darning stitch pattern. (See pages 60–61).

Corner created by darning stitching on a bar and a column pattern.

Linen Sachets

These beautiful sachets are perfect for gift-giving, to wrap small gifts and put them under the tree or as original place card holders for the holiday table.

Cut 20 x 25 cm piece of fabric for each sachet. Make a 2-cm hem along top (25 cm) edge. Fold rectangle in half and press to mark midline. At center of one half (allowing for side seam), embroider a small diamond-shaped design (about 5 to 6 cm across). Cut interior threads and work hemstitch and darning stitch with perle # 5 and gold threads. Frame designs with ribbon borders. Right sides together, refold sachet and sew bottom edges and open side. Turn right side out.

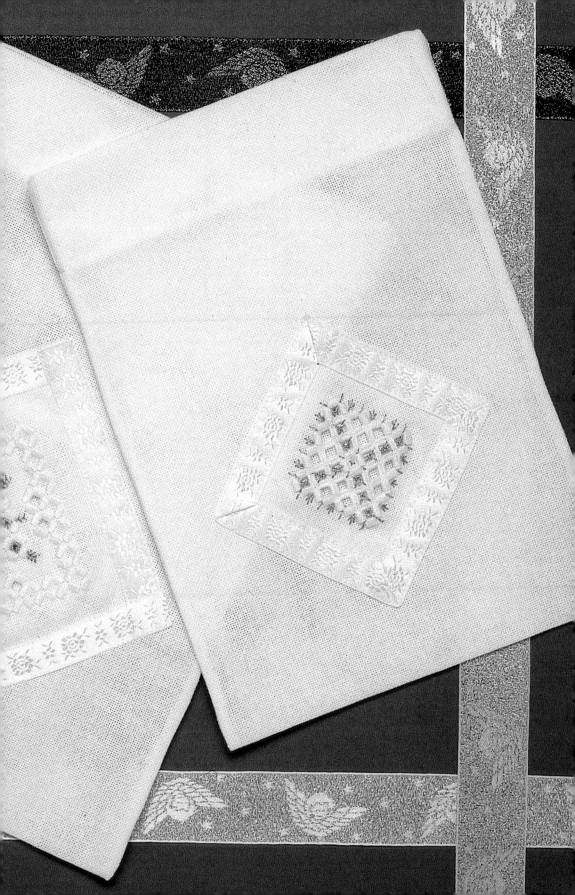

Breakfast Set

This is a beautiful place mat for a modern breakfast table. The set shown here is embroidered with Hardanger kloster patterns on natural linen. The following page shows another traditional pattern.

Place mat. Cut a 45 x 40 cm rectangle. Make a 2-cm border and hemstitch it. Work a kloster block pattern as shown, working in opposite corners with #8 thread.

Napkin. Cut a 25 x 25 cm square and embroider with klosters (#8 thread), darning stitch and dove's eye as shown, using # 25 thread. For napkin ring, cut a 5 x 15 cm rectangle. Work design at center, then hem edges, making a darning stitch loop at one end and sew a button to opposite end.

1 Work the border of the motif by satin stitching the shape of the motif.

2 Pull the threads vertically and horizontally, leaving four threads in the center of each side. Use tweezers to easily remove the threads.

3 At one side of pulled area, wrap top-half of two of unpulled threads to create a bar, ending at edge. Continue wrapping top half of two remaining threads for next bar; then at center corner, darn-stitch this last bar to first two threads (next bar) on adjoining side until first bar is covered and new bar is half covered.

4 Continuing with new bar, repeat last step, working around square until all threads are covered, working last corner by darning over bottom of first bar.

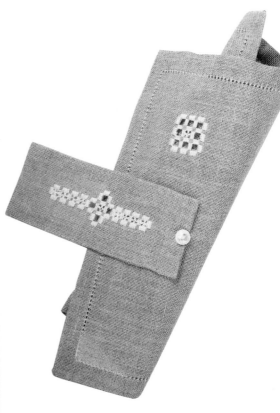

Cute Bookmarks

1–2   To make the top bookmark, trace design shape and embroider the border with festoon stitch, with knot at outer edge. Pull threads (in a pull 4, leave 4 pattern) and cut threads close to border as shown. Leaving thread intersections unworked, darn-stitch the 4-thread bars at center, and work a dove's in empty squares at center. Carefully trim off excess fabric. You can also simply embroider a kloster design and stars within the border (below) without pulling threads. Trim excess fabric and add a fringe to the top.

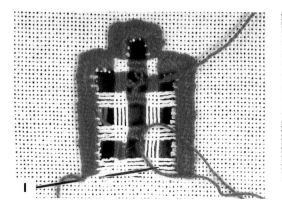

1

2

MEASUREMENTS

Measurements given in this book are given in centimeters. About 2.5 centimeters (abbreviated as *cm*) equal 1 inch. Many tape measures and rulers today show both inches and centimeters, so rather than converting the measurements to inches, simply use the metric side of your measure.

GLOSSARY OF SPECIAL TERMS AND STITCHES

Bare area—Work area where threads have been pulled in one or both directions.

Cording stitch—Wrap the thread around and around the threads of one or more bars. Wrap the same number of times around each bar on any given motif, unless directed otherwise, for uniformity.

Darning stitch—Weave the threaded needle over and under a pair or group of threads or bars drawing them together to form a neat column. Darned bars are also called woven bars.

Festoon stitch—Make a stitch, catching the thread loop with the needle, as in a buttonhole stitch. The small knot formed makes a firm edge and is often used to secure the ends of the work area where threads have been pulled.

Kloster—A solid block formed of satin stitches (usually 5 stitches), with a thread between the stitches (4 threads in a block of 5 stitches).

Matching bars—As hemstitching is worked along the top or the bottom edge of a work area, threads are evenly grouped together in pairs, 3's, 4's, or more. When the opposite edge of the work area is worked and the same threads are grouped at the bottom as at the top, they are said to be matching.

Woven bar—See Darning stitch.